Vegan World Tour XXL

The Best Recipes out of this World

Lydia Solotova

Preface

Discover an exclusive in this unique book collection from 100 vegans dishes from different parts of the world. Some of these delicacies have always been purely plant-based, while others were converted into vegan delights specifically for this book.

During the careful compilation of these recipes, I have deliberately avoided using exotic ingredients to give you an uncomplicated experience to enable simple preparation.

The dishes are deliberately kept simple so that no more excuses stand in the way of the vegan in the kitchen.

Dive into a world of enjoyment, without complex ingredients and with recipes that are easy to follow.
I wish you a lot of Joy in exploring and trying out these diverse options of vegan dishes!

Bon appetit!

Table of contents

Preface..2
In advance - Information about the Recipes..............................6
Starters, Salads and Breakfast..7
    Russian Carrot Salad..8
    Moroccan Couscous Salad...9
    Swedish Oatmeal Porridge...10
    Ukrainian Borscht Omelette...11
    Bulgur Salad "Tabouleh" (Lebanon)..................................12
    Bruschetta with Avocado (Italy)..13
    Green Smoothie - (USA)..14
    Bircher Muesli (Switzerland)..15
    Indian Masala Dosa...16
    Moroccan Shakshuka...17
    Sweet Potato Pastéis de Nata (Portugal)............................18
Soups..19
    Tomato Soup (Italy)..20
    Peanut soup "Mafé" (Senegal/Mali)..................................21
    French Vegetable Soup "Pistou".......................................22
    Pumpkin Cream Soup (Austria).......................................23
    Lentil Soup "Mercimek Çorbası" (Türkiye).......................24
    Spanish Gazpacho (Cold Soup).......................................25
    Potato Soup (Germany)..26
    Baingan Bharta Soup (India)..27
    Greek Bean Soup "Fassolada"..28
    Borscht (Russia)...29
    Erwtensoep (Netherlands)...30
Main Courses..31
    King Pao Tofu Bowl (China)..32
    Vegetable Moussaka (Greece)..33
    Nasi Goreng (Indonesia)...34
    Chop Suey (China)..35
    Chili Sin Carne (Mexico)...36
    Spaghetti Napoli (Italy)...37
    Paella (Spain)...38
    African Kidney Bean Stew...39
    Indian Spiced Rice..40
    Grönsaksbullar (Sweden)...41
    Gemist a (Greece)...42
    Carrot Risotto (Italy)...43

- Cauliflower Gratin (Norway)..44
- Potato rock stomp (Germany)...45
- Indian Curry "Chana Masala"..46
- Ratatouille (France)..47
- Falafel (Lebanon)...48
- Potato Goulash (Hungary)...49
- Sushi (Japan)..50
- Polish Cabbage Stew "Bigos"..51
- Finnish Vegetable Patties..52
- Tomato and Pepper Rice dish (Portugal).................................53
- Kaiserschmarrn (Austria)...54
- White Bean Stew (Bulgaria)...55
- South Tyrolean Spinach Dumplings (Italy)............................56
- Potato Gratin (France)..57
- Couscous with Chickpeas (Morocco).......................................58
- Grilled Green Asparagus (Spain)...59
- Fried Rice (Vietnam)...60
- Vegetable Stew "Chakalaka" (South Africa)..........................61
- Tempeh Pan (Indonesia)...62
- Rösti with Vegetables (Switzerland)..63
- Glass Noodles "Japchae" (Korea)...64
- Braised White Cabbage (Ukraine)...65
- Massaman Curry (Thailand)..66
- Tofu Noodles with Teriyaki Sauce (Japan)............................67
- Mac 'n' Cheese (USA)..68
- Sauces, Dips, Dressings and Spreads..69
  - Hummus (Syria)..70
  - Peanut Butter (USA)..71
  - Alioli (Spain)...72
  - Guacamole (Mexico)...73
  - Muhammara (Syrian)...74
  - Macadamia Mint Pesto (Australia)...75
  - Vegan Liver Sausage (Germany)...76
  - Greek Feta...77
  - Greek Tzatziki..78
  - Italian Pesto..79
  - Gochujang Sauce (Korea)..80
  - Arrabbiata Sauce (Italy)..81
  - Sate Sauce (Indonesia)...82
  - Curry Coconut Sauce (India)..83
- Bread and Buns..84

- Baguette (France)...85
- Ciabatta (Italy)...86
- Swiss Bürli..87
- Indian Naan Rolls...88
- Mexican Tortillas..89
- Rolls (Germany)...90
- Chinese Mantou...91
- English Scones...92
- Turkish Flatbread...93
- Greek Pita..94
- Desserts and Sweets..95
  - Oat Cookies (Sweden)......................................96
  - Waffles (Belgium)...97
  - Crepes (France)..98
  - American Pancakes..99
  - Almond Tartlets (Spain)..................................100
  - American Lemon Donuts...............................101
  - Sweet Couscous (North Africa).....................102
  - Berry Crumble (England)..............................103
  - Chocolate Chia Pudding (Australia)..............104
  - Panna Cotta (Italy)...105
  - Brownies (USA)..106
  - Mousse au Chocolat (France).......................107
  - Dulce de Leche (Argentina)..........................108
  - Chocolate Ice Cream (Italy)..........................109
  - Blueberry Cassis – Lassi (India)...................110
  - Popcorn with Caramel Sauce (USA).............111
- Disclaimer..112
- Imprint...113

In advance - Information about the Recipes

- The specified baking times come from my oven. Please note that deviations can often occur here.
- If you use top/bottom heat, increase the temperature by 20 degrees Celsius.
- All recipes can be changed according to your own wishes.
- Vegetables should always be purchased in organic quality.
- Always wash vegetables. I haven't specified that in the recipes.
- Of course, you can also use fresh seasoning instead of powder seasoning.
- Instead of vegan butter, vegan margarine can be used at any time.
- Instead of one dice of yeast, 2 packets of dry yeast can be used.
- Instead of sugar, naturally Xylitol or cane sugar can also be used.

Recipe - Ingredients every vegan needs

- nutritional yeast
- Kala Namak salt
- Agave syrup

Abbreviations

- TK = frozen
- tsp = teaspoon
- tbsp= tablespoon

Starters, Salads and Breakfast

Appetite stimulant, Fresh kicks and morning joys:
Start your day with tempting starters, refreshing
salads and irresistible breakfast ideas!

Russian Carrot Salad

Ingredients

1 kg carrots
1 clove of garlic
1 tbsp vinegar
1 teaspoon salt
1 tsp sugar

1 onion
100 ml (rapeseed) oil
1 tsp salt
1 teaspoon coriander

Preparation

Grate carrots and mix with vinegar.
Press the garlic clove and dice the onion into small pieces.
Heat oil in a pot.
Add onion and garlic and fry over medium heat for 3 minutes.
Pour the contents of the pot over the carrots and mix with the remaining ingredients.
Allow to steep for 15 minutes before serving.

Moroccan Couscous Salad

Ingredients

100 g couscous
1/2 can chickpeas (rinsed)
1/2 cucumber, diced
2 tbsp dried apricots, diced
2 tbsp coarsely chopped roasted almonds

180 ml vegetable broth
1 red pepper, diced
2 tbsp chopped mint
2 tbsp chopped parsley

For the dressing:
2 tbsp olive oil
½ tsp ground cumin
Salt and pepper to taste

1 tbsp lemon juice
½ tsp agave syrup

Preparation

Pour boiling vegetable broth over the couscous, cover and let it soak for 10 minutes.

Mix the dressing made from olive oil, lemon juice, cumin, agave syrup, salt and pepper.

Fluff up the swollen couscous and let it cool.

Add chickpeas, peppers, cucumber, apricots, mint, parsley and almonds.

Pour the dressing over the salad and mix carefully. Cool in the refrigerator before serving, optionally garnish with fresh mint and parsley.

Swedish Oatmeal Porridge

Ingredients

100 g oat flakes
500 ml almond milk (or another plant-based milk of your choice)
Fresh berries or fruit as desired
Chopped nuts (e.g., almonds or walnuts)
Maple syrup or agave syrup to sweeten (optional)
A pinch of salt

Preparation

Mix the oat flakes, almond milk and a pinch of salt in a saucepan.

Place the pot over medium heat and bring the mixture to a boil.

Once the porridge is boiling, reduce the heat and simmer the mixture, stirring occasionally, until the oats are soft and a creamy consistency is formed (usually about 5-7 minutes).

Remove the porridge from the heat and let it rest briefly. If necessary, sweeten it with maple syrup or agave syrup.

Pour the porridge into bowls and garnish with fresh berries or your favorite fruit. Sprinkle chopped nuts over the porridge to add a pleasant crunch.

Ukrainian Borscht Omelette

Ingredients

120 g chickpea flour
120 ml beetroot juice
Mixed mushrooms as desired
Fresh herbs for garnish

Preparation

Mix chickpea flour with beetroot juice.
Fry the mushrooms in a pan and pour the chickpea mixture over them.
Fry until golden brown and garnish with fresh herbs.

Bulgur Salad "Tabouleh" (Lebanon)

Ingredients

150 g bulgur
1 bunch of fresh parsley, finely chopped
½ bunch fresh mint, finely chopped
3 tablespoons olive oil
2 large tomatoes, diced
½ cucumber, diced
Juice of 2 lemons
Salt and pepper

Preparation

Cook bulgur according to package instructions and allow to cool.
Place tomatoes, parsley, mint and cucumber in a large bowl.
Add cooled bulgur.
Drizzle lemon juice and olive oil over it, mix well.
Season with salt and pepper.
Let sit in the fridge for at least 15 minutes before serving.

Bruschetta with Avocado (Italy)

Ingredients

Baguette, sliced
2 tomatoes, dice
Fresh basil
Salt and pepper to taste

2 ripe avocados, mashed
2 garlic, chopped
3 tablespoons olive oil, for drizzling

Preparation

Lightly toast the baguette slices.
Spread avocado on the roasted slices.
Garnish with diced tomatoes, garlic and basil.
Drizzle with olive oil and season with salt and pepper.

Green Smoothie - (USA)

Ingredients (2 servings)

1 banana
1 apple
300 ml water
150 g frozen baby spinach (if fresh, add 50 g ice cubes)

Preparation

Core the apple.
Puree all ingredients in a blender or a large bowl with a hand blender.
Pour into glasses and serve.
This basic recipe can of course be modified.
If necessary, add raspberries.
A smoothie can also be very thick. The smoothie should actually be spooned like yogurt.

Bircher Muesli (Switzerland)

Ingredients (2 servings)

50 g oat flakes
60 g plant milk (as desired)
Juice from one lemon

60 g water
3 apples
20 g of nuts

Preparation

Mix the oat flakes with water and let it soak overnight.
Add plant milk and lemon juice.
Finely grate or mix apples and nuts and stir in.

Indian Masala Dosa

Ingredients (4 servings)

250 g dosa batter (rice and urdal batter)
300 g boiled potatoes, diced and seasoned with cumin and turmeric
150 g tomato chutney
150g coconut chutney
Fresh coriander leaves

Preparation

Spread dosa batter thinly on a pan and fry until golden brown.
Place seasoned potatoes on one side of the dosa and fold over.
Serve with tomato chutney, coconut chutney and fresh coriander leaves.

Moroccan Shakshuka

Ingredients (4 servings)

400 g tomatoes, diced
150 g onions, chopped
200 g chickpeas, cooked
2 tbsp olive oil
Pita bread for serving

200 g peppers, diced
2 tsp harissa spice
1 teaspoon Ras el Hanout
40 g chickpea flour

Preparation

Heat olive oil in a pan.
Add onions, peppers and tomatoes and sauté over medium heat.
Stir in harissa seasoning and ras el hanout.
Fold in the cooked chickpeas and mix everything well.
Mix chickpea flour with water to create an egg texture, making small wells in the mixture for the "eggs."
Cover the pan and poach the vegan "eggs" until they reach the desired firmness.
Season with salt and pepper.
Serve with pita bread and enjoy.

Sweet Potato Pastéis de Nata (Portugal)

Ingredients

1 pack (approx. 230 g) puff pastry (vegan)
400 g sweet potatoes, peeled and diced
240 ml coconut milk
100 g sugar
1 teaspoon vanilla extract
Cinnamon for sprinkling

Preparation

Lay out the puff pastry in muffin tins and preheat the oven to 200 degrees Celsius.

Boil sweet potato cubes in water until soft. Drain and puree.

Add coconut milk, sugar and vanilla extract to the pureed sweet potatoes and mix well.

Fill the puff pastry molds with the sweet potato mixture.

Bake in the preheated oven for 15-20 minutes until the dough is golden brown.

Sprinkle with cinnamon and allow to cool before serving.

Soups

Enjoyable wake-up calls and refreshing fillers to fall in love with: Start your day with delicious soups in a purely plant-based variety!

Tomato Soup (Italy)

Ingredients

400g chopped tomatoes (or fresh of course)
250 ml vegetable stock   1 onion, finely chopped
1 clove of garlic, pressed   ½ bunch of basil
2 pinches chili   2 pinches pepper
125 g white bread, cut into cubes 2 tbsp olive oil

Preparation

Heat the oil in a pot and fry the onion and garlic until translucent.
Add the tomatoes, chili, salt and pepper to the vegetable stock and bring to the boil.
Simmer on medium heat for 15 minutes.
Add white bread cubes and basil and simmer on medium heat for another 10 minutes.
Stir the soup through and remove from the heat.
Let it steep for 45 minutes and warm it up again before eating.
Serve in deep plates drizzled with olive oil.

Peanut soup "Mafé" (Senegal/Mali)

Ingredients

200 g peanut butter
1 large onion, chopped
1 sweet potato, diced
1 cup okra, sliced
1 liter vegetable broth
1 teaspoon cumin
1 teaspoon paprika powder
Salt and pepper
2 tbsp vegetable oil

1 can chopped tomatoes (400 g)
2 cloves of garlic, chopped
1 eggplant, diced

Preparation

Pour oil into a pan and fry onion with garlic.

Add peanut butter and mix well.

Add vegetables, tomatoes and spices.

Deglaze with vegetable broth and simmer for 30-40 minutes until the vegetables are soft.

French Vegetable Soup "Pistou"

Ingredients

100 g short hollow noodles
1 can chopped tomatoes
100g green beans, cut 1cm long
100 g savoy cabbage, cut into fine strips
1 onion, finely chopped
2 tbsp tomato paste
Salt and pepper
2 tbsp (rapeseed) oil

1 liter vegetable broth
1 carrot, diced
1 zucchini, diced

Preparation

Heat oil in a pot and sauté the onion in it.
Add the savoy cabbage and green beans and sauté briefly.
Stir in the tomato paste and deglaze with vegetable stock and chopped tomatoes.
Add the noodles and simmer for 10 minutes, stirring occasionally.
Add the zucchini and simmer for another 5 minutes.
Season with salt and pepper.

Pumpkin Cream Soup (Austria)

Ingredients

800 g Hokkaido pumpkin, diced
2 potatoes, peeled and diced
1 garlic clove, chopped
200 ml vegetable cooking cream
Salt and pepper to taste
White bread

1 onion, chopped
1 carrot, diced
1 liter vegetable broth
2 tbsp pumpkin seed oil
1 teaspoon cumin (optional)

Preparation

Sauté the onion and garlic in a little oil in a large pot until translucent.

Add pumpkin, potatoes and carrot and fry briefly.

Deglaze with vegetable broth and bring to the boil. Then reduce the heat and simmer until the vegetables are soft.

Puree the soup with a hand blender until it is creamy.

Stir in the vegetable cooking cream and season with salt, pepper and optionally cumin.

Before serving, garnish with a splash of pumpkin seed oil and serve with white bread.

Lentil Soup "Mercimek Çorbası" (Türkiye)

Ingredients

200 g red lentils, washed and drained
1 onion, finely chopped
1 potato, diced
1 teaspoon paprika powder
1.5 liters vegetable broth
slices for serving
Fresh parsley for garnish

1 carrot, diced
1 teaspoon cumin
3 tbsp tomato paste
3 tablespoons olive oil
Salt and pepper Lemon

Preparation

Heat the oil in a large pot and sauté the chopped onion until translucent. Add carrots and potatoes and fry briefly.

Add tomato paste, paprika powder and cumin. Mix everything well and let it cook for about 2 minutes.

Add the washed lentils and pour in vegetable stock or water.

Bring the soup to a boil and then reduce the heat. Simmer for about 20-25 minutes until the lentils and vegetables are soft.

Puree the soup until it reaches a creamy consistency.

Season with salt and pepper. Serve with lemon slices and fresh parsley.

Spanish Gazpacho (Cold Soup)

Ingredients

6 ripe tomatoes, diced

1 red pepper, deseeded and diced

2 cloves garlic, minced

4 tablespoons olive oil

2 slices of stale bread, cut into cubes

Salt and pepper to taste

Fresh basil leaves for garnish

1 cucumber, peeled and diced

1 small onion, roughly chopped

4 cups tomato juice

2 tablespoons white wine vinegar

Preparation

Place tomatoes, cucumber, peppers, onion and garlic in a blender.

Add tomato juice, olive oil and white wine vinegar.

Add stale bread to the mixture and puree everything into a creamy soup.

Season gazpacho with salt and pepper.

Chill the soup in the refrigerator for at least 2 hours to allow the flavors to develop.

Garnish with fresh basil before serving.

Serve cold and enjoy. Optionally drizzle with a drizzle of olive oil.

Potato Soup (Germany)

Ingredients

500g potatoes, peeled and diced
1 onion, chopped
2 cloves of garlic, minced
1 leek, cut into rings
250 ml vegetable cooking cream
1 bay leaf
Fresh parsley for garnish

2 carrots, diced
1 stick of celery, diced
1 liter vegetable broth
2 tbsp vegetable oil
1 teaspoon thyme
Salt and pepper to taste.

Preparation

Heat oil in a large pot and sauté onions with garlic until translucent. Add carrots, celery and leeks. Sauté briefly until the vegetables are lightly browned. Add potatoes and deglaze with vegetable broth.

Add bay leaf, thyme, salt and pepper. Bring the soup to a boil and then reduce the heat.

Simmer the soup for 20-25 minutes until the vegetables are soft.

Stir in the vegetable cooking cream and bring to the boil briefly.

Remove the bay leaf and mix the soup until creamy with a hand blender. Season with salt and pepper.

Garnish with fresh parsley and serve.

Baingan Bharta Soup (India)

Ingredients

1 large eggplant (approx. 400 g)
1 onion, chopped
1 teaspoon ginger, grated
1 teaspoon garam masala
1 teaspoon paprika powder
2 tbsp vegetable oil
Fresh coriander leaves for garnish

2 tomatoes, diced
2 cloves of garlic, chopped
1 teaspoon cumin
1 teaspoon turmeric
1 liter vegetable broth
Salt and pepper

Preparation

Roast the eggplant, remove the skin and roughly chop the flesh.
Fry onion, garlic and ginger in oil.
Add spices and roast briefly.
Add tomatoes until soft.
Add chopped eggplant pulp and stir.
Deglaze with vegetable broth and simmer for 15-20 minutes.
Season with salt and pepper.
Garnish with fresh coriander before serving.

Greek Bean Soup "Fassolada"

Ingredients

250 g white beans, dried (previously soaked and cooked)
1 onion, chopped
2 celery sticks, diced
3 cloves of garlic, chopped
2 tbsp tomato paste
1 tsp dried oregano
1 liter vegetable broth

2 carrots, diced
3 tomatoes, diced
1 bay leaf
3 tbsp olive oil
Salt and pepper
Fresh parsley for garnish

Preparation

Drain the soaked and cooked beans.

Heat the olive oil in a large pot and sauté the onions, celery and carrots until soft.

Add garlic and continue to fry briefly.

Stir in diced tomatoes and tomato paste and continue cooking until tomatoes break down.

Add the drained beans, bay leaf and oregano.

Deglaze with vegetable broth and bring to the boil.

Reduce the heat and simmer the soup until the beans and vegetables are tender, about 30-40 minutes. Season with salt and pepper and serve garnished with fresh parsley.

Borscht (Russia)

Ingredients

250 g beetroot, peeled and diced
1 onion, chopped
1/2 white cabbage, finely chopped
1 garlic clove, chopped
2 tbsp tomato paste
2 bay leaves
Salt and pepper to taste.
Vegan sour cream (optional)

1 potato (approx. 150 g), diced
1 carrot, diced
2 tomatoes, diced
1 liter vegetable broth
2 tbsp vegetable oil
1 teaspoon vinegar
Fresh parsley for garnish

Preparation

Heat the oil in a pot and sauté the onions and garlic until translucent.

Add beetroot, potatoes, carrots, white cabbage and tomatoes and fry briefly.

Deglaze with vegetable broth, add bay leaves and bring to the boil.

Reduce heat, stir in tomato paste and vinegar. Simmer the soup for 20-25 minutes until the vegetables are soft.

Season with salt and pepper.

Garnish with fresh parsley before serving.

Serve with a dollop of vegan sour cream if desired.

Erwtensoep (Netherlands)

Ingredients

250g dried green peas, soaked overnight
1 onion, chopped
2 carrots, diced (approx. 200 g)
1 leek, cut into rings
2 bay leaves
1 tsp marjoram
Salt and pepper to taste.

2 potatoes, diced (approx. 300 g)
1 celery stick, diced
2 cloves of garlic, chopped
1 teaspoon thyme
2 liters vegetable broth
Fresh parsley for garnish

Preparation

Rinse and drain the soaked peas.

In a large pot, sauté the onions and garlic in a little oil until translucent.

Add potatoes, carrots, celery and leek and fry briefly.

Add the soaked peas, bay leaves, thyme, marjoram and vegetable stock.

Bring to a boil and then reduce the heat. Simmer the soup for about 1.5 hours until the peas and vegetables are soft.

Remove the bay leaves and puree some of the soup with an immersion blender to obtain a thicker consistency.

Season with salt and pepper.

Serve garnished with fresh parsley.

Main Courses

Culinary wake-up calls and filling treats that will make your heartbeat faster: Start your day with delicate main dishes from a variety of purely plant-based delights!

King Pao Tofu Bowl (China)

Ingredients

200 g firm tofu, diced
2 tablespoons soy sauce
1 tbsp rice vinegar
1 tbsp agave syrup
1 tbsp cornstarch
2 tbsp peanut oil
2 cloves garlic, minced
1 teaspoon fresh ginger, grated
1 red pepper, diced
1 yellow pepper, diced
1 cup broccoli florets
½ cup unsalted peanuts
Spring onions, cut into rings, for garnish
Cooked basmati rice or quinoa, as a side dish

For the sauce:
3 tbsp soy sauce
2 tbsp rice vinegar
1 tbsp agave syrup
1 tsp cornstarch
1 tsp Sriracha (optional for spiciness)

Preparation

Marinate tofu cubes in soy sauce, rice vinegar, maple syrup and corn starch, let sit for at least 15 minutes. Heat peanut oil in a pan, fry the tofu cubes until golden brown, then set aside. Fry the garlic and ginger in a pan until fragrant, briefly add the peppers, broccoli and peanuts until the vegetables are crispy. Add marinated tofu cubes back to the pan. Mix the sauce from soy sauce, rice vinegar, maple syrup, corn starch and optionally Sriracha, pour over the tofu-vegetable mixture and mix well. Remove the pan from the heat when the sauce has thickened. Garnish with spring onions and serve over cooked basmati rice or quinoa.

Vegetable Moussaka (Greece)

Ingredients

2 eggplants
4 potatoes
3 cloves of garlic
125 g tomato paste
1 teaspoon dried thyme
60 g breadcrumbs
480 ml soy milk
A pinch of nutmeg,

2 zucchini
1 onion
400 g diced tomatoes
1 teaspoon dried oregano
1 teaspoon paprika powder
60 ml olive oil
30 g flour
Salt and pepper

Preparation

Cut the eggplant, zucchini and potatoes into thin slices.

Fry the eggplant slices and drain on kitchen paper.

Pre-cook the potato slices, drain and set aside.

Fry onions and garlic in olive oil, add tomatoes, tomato paste, spices and simmer for 15 minutes.

Mix soy milk, flour, nutmeg in a pot and allow to thicken. Grease the baking dish, pour in layers of potatoes, eggplant, zucchini and tomato sauce.

Pour bechamel sauce over it and sprinkle with breadcrumbs.

Bake at 180 degrees Celsius for 45-50 minutes.

Allow to cool and cut into pieces before serving.

Nasi Goreng (Indonesia)

Ingredients

300 g cooked rice (preferably chilled and from the day before)
200 g vegetables (peas, carrots, spring onions), diced
150g fried tofu, diced
2 tbsp soy sauce
1 tbsp Kecap Manis (sweet soy sauce)
Salt and pepper to taste
Fresh coriander leaves for garnish

2 cloves of garlic, minced
1 tsp sambal oelek (chilli paste)
2 tbsp vegetable oil

Preparation

Heat the oil in a pan. Fry the garlic until fragrant.
Add vegetables and sauté briefly until slightly soft.
Add tofu and mix.
Add the cooked rice to the pan and mix thoroughly with the other ingredients.
Add soy sauce, kecap manis and sambal oelek. Stir everything well.
If necessary, add salt and pepper to taste.
Serve on plates and garnish with fresh coriander leaves.

Chop Suey (China)

Ingredients

2 peppers
100 g broccoli
1 onion
½ glass of bean sprouts
200 ml water
2 tbsp sugar
1 teaspoon paprika
Side dish: rice

150 g cauliflower
3 carrots
100 g mushrooms
6 mini corn cobs
100 ml soy sauce
½ tsp ginger
3 tablespoons (sesame) oil for frying

Preparation

Cut vegetables (peppers, mushrooms, onion, cauliflower, broccoli and carrots) into bite-sized pieces. Drain the bean sprouts. Halve mini corn cobs lengthwise and crosswise. Let the cauliflower and broccoli steep in hot water.

Bring 150 ml water, soy sauce, sugar, ginger and paprika powder to the boil in a pot. Dissolve starch in 50 ml water and slowly stir into the sauce. Bring to the boil briefly, then simmer over low heat.

Heat oil in a pan. Fry carrots first, after 2 minutes add peppers, mushrooms, cauliflower and broccoli. After another 2 minutes, add mini corn cobs and bean sprouts and fry briefly. Mix the vegetables with the sauce and simmer briefly over a low heat (vegetables should still be al dente). Serve on warmed plates with rice.

Chili Sin Carne (Mexico)

Ingredients

120 g soy granules
400 g chopped tomatoes
1 can of kidney beans (drained weight 240g)
1 can of corn
2 cloves of garlic
1 teaspoon chili powder
3 pinches of pepper
1 piece of vegan dark chocolate

500 ml vegetable broth
1 pepper

1 onion
2 tablespoons of tomato paste
3 pinches of salt
Optional 100g soy cream
2 tablespoons (rapeseed) oil for frying

Side dish: vegan tortilla chips

Preparation

Soak the soy granules in hot vegetable broth, drain and drain. Reserve cooking liquid. Dice the onion, deseed the peppers and dice them too. Press the garlic, drain the kidney beans and corn. Heat oil in a large pot. Fry the soy granules, onion and peppers over medium heat for 5 minutes. Add tomatoes, tomato paste, garlic, chili powder, salt and pepper and simmer for 15 minutes. Add kidney beans, corn and chocolate, simmer for another 5 minutes. If necessary, top up the chili with the reserved cooking liquid and bring to the boil again. Optionally stir in soy cream, bring to the boil and let it simmer over low heat for 3 minutes. Serve with tortilla chips. The chili develops its full flavor best if it has been steeped for a day and then reheated before serving.

Spaghetti Napoli (Italy)

Ingredients

500 g spaghetti (without egg)
1 onion
1 bunch of basil
2 pinches of pepper
5 liters of water

2 cans of pureed tomatoes
2 cloves of garlic
80 ml olive oil
2 tbsp salt
Optional yeast flakes

Preparation

Bring 5 liters of water to the boil in a large pot. Add 2 tbsp salt. Cook spaghetti according to package instructions (6-8 minutes) on medium heat.

In the meantime, chop onions and press garlic. Heat oil in a deep pan. Fry onions and garlic until translucent.

Add tomatoes and cook over medium heat for 10 minutes while stirring.

Add salt, pepper and oil. Tear the basil leaves into small pieces and mix with the sauce.

When the spaghetti is al dente, drain and add to the sauce. Season to taste. Use yeast flakes as a substitute for Parmesan.

Paella (Spain)

Ingredients

200 g basmati rice
80 ml white wine
2 cloves of garlic
100g green beans
80 ml (olive oil
1 pinch of chili powder
2 pinches of cinnamon
1 teaspoon salt

500 ml vegetable broth
1 onion
2 peppers (color of your choice)
100g peas
1 teaspoon paprika powder
1 pinch of rosemary
1 teaspoon of lemon juice
½ lemon to decorate.

Preparation

Press the garlic, chop the onion, beans and peppers into small pieces.

Heat the oil in a large pan and fry the garlic cloves with the onion and pepper over medium heat for 3 minutes.

Stir in the unwashed rice and sauté for another 2 minutes. Add vegetable broth, white wine, lemon juice and cinnamon and simmer on low heat for 15 minutes. Stir in the beans and peas and simmer on low for another 15 minutes.

Stir in salt, chili powder, rosemary and paprika powder.

Garnish with lemon slices on preheated plates.

African Kidney Bean Stew

Ingredients

250g dried green peas, soaked overnight
1 can kidney beans
5 tomatoes
1 tbsp peanut butter
1 teaspoon cumin
(Rapeseed) oil for frying,

2 onions
3 cloves of garlic
2 tsp sambal oelek
1 pinch of salt
parsley for sprinkling

Side dish: rice

Preparation

Drain the kidney beans and wash them thoroughly. Finely dice the onion, press the garlic cloves and cut the tomatoes into cubes.

Heat oil in a pot and sauté onions until translucent. Add tomatoes and simmer over medium heat for 5 minutes.

Add garlic, salt, sambal oelek, kidney beans and cumin. Add peanut butter and bring to the boil briefly.

Simmer over medium heat for 3 minutes.

Serve with rice and sprinkle with some parsley.

Indian Spiced Rice

Ingredients

350 g basmati rice
1 teaspoon ginger
1 tsp cardamom
1 tbsp parsley
800 ml water
4 tbsp (rapeseed) oil for frying

1 teaspoon chili
1 teaspoon cinnamon
1 tsp coriander
½ tsp cumin
3 pinches of salt

Preparation

Heat 2 tablespoons of oil in a pot, add the washed rice.
Fry the rice until translucent, stirring constantly.
Add all ingredients except the remaining oil and the parsley. Bring to the boil and then simmer covered at the lowest setting for 20 minutes.
Remove the lid, turn off the stove.
After 2 minutes, fold in the remaining oil and parsley.
Serve in warm plates.

Grönsaksbullar (Sweden)

Ingredients

200 g mixed vegetables (carrots, peas, corn), finely diced
200 g potatoes, cooked and mashed
1 onion, finely chopped
Salt and pepper to taste
150 g oat flakes
2 tbsp soy sauce
2 tablespoons vegetable oil (for frying)

For the mustard dill sauce:
100 g vegan mayonnaise
1 tbsp fresh dill, finely chopped
1 tbsp Dijon mustard
salt and pepper

Preparation

Fry the mixed vegetables in a pan with a little oil until soft. Set aside and let cool.

In a bowl, combine the boiled and mashed potatoes, oatmeal, chopped onion, soy sauce and sautéed vegetables. Season with salt and pepper. Form small balls out of the mixture.

Heat the vegetable oil in a pan and fry the vegetable balls over medium heat until golden brown.

For the mustard-dill sauce, mix all the ingredients well and season with salt and pepper.

Arrange the vegetable balls on a plate and serve with the mustard-dill sauce.

Gemist a (Greece)

Ingredients

4 large tomatoes
250 g rice
1 garlic clove, chopped
100 g tomato paste
1 tsp dried dill
500 ml vegetable broth

4 peppers
1 onion, finely chopped
120 ml olive oil
1 teaspoon dried oregano
salt and pepper

Preparation

Cook the rice according to package instructions.

Cut off the tops of the tomatoes and hollow out the insides. Halve the peppers and remove the seeds.

Sauté onion and garlic in olive oil. Add tomato paste, oregano, dill, salt and pepper. Stir in the cooked rice.

Stuff the vegetable mixture into the prepared tomato and pepper halves.

Place stuffed vegetables in a baking dish. Add vegetable broth.

Bake in a preheated oven at 180 degrees Celsius for about 45 minutes until the vegetables are soft.

Carrot Risotto (Italy)

Ingredients

500 g risotto rice
1 onion
1 liter vegetable broth
1 tbsp parsley
3 pinches of pepper
3 tablespoons olive oil for frying

5 carrots
1 clove of garlic
250 ml white wine
1 tsp lemon juice
3 pinches of salt

Preparation

Prepare vegetable broth in a pot and keep warm.

Dice the onion small, press the garlic clove and cut the carrots into fine sticks.

Heat 2 tablespoons of oil in a pot and fry the onion and garlic until translucent.

Add the rice and sauté briefly and deglaze with wine.

Add the carrots and simmer over medium heat for 5 minutes.

Add the vegetable stock and simmer until the risotto is soft but still has a bite.

Stir in the remaining oil with the parsley, lemon juice, salt and pepper.

Serve in deep plates.

Cauliflower Gratin (Norway)

Ingredients

1 medium-sized cauliflower (approx. 800 g)

200 g vegan cheese sauce

2 tablespoons vegetable margarine

1 tsp mustard

150 g vegan grated cheese

200 ml oat milk

2 tbsp flour

Salt and pepper to taste

1 tbsp chopped parsley (optional)

Preparation

Cut the cauliflower into small florets and cook in lightly salted water until just tender. Drain.

Melt margarine in a pot, add flour and sauté briefly. Slowly stir in oat milk until a smooth sauce forms.

Add vegan cheese sauce and mix well. Stir in mustard, salt and pepper.

Place the cauliflower in a baking dish, pour the cheese sauce over it and spread it evenly.

Sprinkle vegan grated cheese on top.

Bake in a preheated oven at 200 degrees Celsius for about 20 minutes until the cheese is golden brown.

Garnish with chopped parsley if desired and serve.

Potato rock stomp (Germany)

Ingredients

800 g potatoes, peeled and diced
2 tbsp vegetable margarine
2 tbsp plant-based milk
Fried onions for sprinkling

200 g fresh spinach
1 onion, finely chopped
Salt and pepper

Preparation

Boil the potato cubes in a pot of salted water until tender. Drain and return to the pot.
In a separate pot, sauté the spinach until wilted.
Melt vegetable margarine in a pan and fry the onion until golden brown.
Mash the cooked potatoes, add non-dairy milk and mix well.
Fold the steamed spinach and roasted onions into the mashed potatoes.
Season with salt and pepper.
Spread the mashed potatoes on plates and sprinkle with fried onions.

Indian Curry "Chana Masala"

Ingredients

400 g chickpeas (canned), rinsed and drained
2 tbsp vegetable oil   150 g onion, finely chopped
15g garlic, chopped   15g fresh ginger, grated
1 green chili, chopped (optional for spiciness)
1 teaspoon cumin   1 teaspoon coriander powder
½ tsp turmeric   1 tsp garam masala
1 tsp paprika   120 ml water
400 g chopped tomatoes (canned)   Salt and pepper
Fresh coriander for garnish

Preparation

Heat the oil in a large pot and fry the chopped onion until golden brown. Add garlic, ginger and green chilli (if using), fry for another 2 minutes.

Stir in cumin, coriander powder, turmeric, garam masala and paprika and sauté for 1 minute. Add the chopped tomatoes and mix everything well. Let simmer for about 5 minutes.

Add the rinsed chickpeas, water, salt and pepper. Stir well and simmer over medium heat for 15-20 minutes.

Garnish with fresh coriander and serve with rice or naan bread.

Ratatouille (France)

Ingredients

5 tomatoes, sliced
1 zucchini, diced
2 onions, finely chopped
1 teaspoon thyme
1 teaspoon basil
1 tbsp olive oil

2 eggplants, diced
3 peppers, diced
2 cloves of garlic, pressed
1 teaspoon parsley
2 pinches pepper

Preparation

Heat oil in a pot and fry onion and garlic until translucent.

Add the tomatoes, peppers and all the spices and simmer for 10 minutes at medium heat, stirring occasionally.

Add the eggplant and zucchini and cook, stirring occasionally, for another 15 minutes.

Serve with fresh baguette.

Falafel (Lebanon)

Ingredients

120 g chickpea flour
2 cloves of garlic, pressed
1 tbsp parsley
½ tsp cumin
1 teaspoon olive oil
Olive oil for frying

1 onion, finely diced
200 ml water
1 tsp salt
½ tsp lemon juice
1 pinch of baking powder

Preparation

Bring water to a boil in a pot.
Mix all dry ingredients together and pour boiling water over them.
Mix well and let soak for 15 minutes.
Mix dough with lemon juice and oil.
Heat oil in a pan.
Form the falafel with moistened hands and fry over medium heat.
If possible, only turn once and fry covered.

Potato Goulash (Hungary)

Ingredients

2 potatoes
1 onion
2 cloves of garlic
1 tsp caraway
2 teaspoons paprika
3 pinches of chili powder
Water to cover the potatoes

250 g mushrooms
2 red peppers
2 teaspoons of tomato paste
1 tsp marjoram
Salt and pepper
4 tablespoons of rapeseed oil for frying

Preparation

Finely chop the onion, press the garlic cloves, cut the mushrooms into pieces, and slice the peppers and potatoes.

Heat 2 tablespoons of oil in a pot and fry the onion over medium heat until translucent.

Stir in the tomato paste and after 1 minute add the potatoes, peppers and garlic. After 3 minutes, add enough water to cover the potatoes.

Add remaining ingredients and simmer until soft for 10 minutes.

If too much water evaporates, perhaps add a little more water. Heat the remaining oil in a pan and fry the mushrooms until golden brown. Stir the mushrooms into the goulash and serve in preheated plates.

Sushi (Japan)

Ingredients

2 nori seaweed sheets
2 tbsp rice vinegar
1 carrot, chopped
½ cucumber, deseeded and cut into thin strips
A pinch of salt
Ginger and wasabi to taste
200 g sushi rice
1 tbsp sugar
½ avocado, thinly sliced
Soy sauce to serve

Preparation

Cook sushi rice according to package directions.

In a small bowl, combine rice vinegar, sugar and salt. Place the cooked rice in a large bowl and fold in the vinegar mixture. Let cool down.

Place a nori sheet on a bamboo mat. Spread a thin layer of rice evenly over the nori, leaving a border of about 1 cm at the top. Place the vegetable strips and avocado slices horizontally on the bottom edge of the rice.

Roll up the bamboo mat from the bottom, making sure that the filling is wrapped tightly.

Moisten the free edge of the nori with a little water and roll up the roll completely. Place the roll, seam side down, on a cutting board.

Cut the roll into about 6-8 pieces with a sharp knife.

Serve the sushi pieces with soy sauce, ginger and wasabi.

Polish Cabbage Stew "Bigos"

Ingredients

400 g natural tofu
400 g mushrooms
1 onion
2 bay leaves
1 tbsp vegetable broth
Salt and pepper to taste
Side dish: bread

1 small head of white cabbage
1 sauerkraut packet
1 ½ tubes of tomato paste
4 juniper berries
1 tsp paprika powder
4 tablespoons rapeseed oil for frying

Preparation

Dry the tofu well with kitchen paper and cut into cubes.

Cut the white cabbage into fine strips, chop the mushrooms and onion into small pieces.

Heat 2 tablespoons of oil in a pot and sauté the white cabbage, sauerkraut, bay leaves and juniper berries until the white cabbage is al dente. Heat remaining oil in a pan.

Fry the onion and mushrooms for 5 minutes over medium heat.

Add the tofu, vegetable broth and spices and fry until the tofu turns golden brown.

When the white cabbage is al dente, stir in the tomato paste and add the tofu pan to the pot and mix well. Serve with bread. By the way, Bigos tastes best when it has been steeped for a day and heated again.

Finnish Vegetable Patties

Ingredients

100 g oat flakes
2 large potatoes, boiled and mashed
1 onion, finely chopped
1 teaspoon ground cumin
Salt and pepper to taste
3 tablespoons flour (for consistency)

1 carrot, finely grated
2 cloves of garlic, pressed
1 teaspoon paprika powder
2 tablespoons of tomato paste
oil for frying

Preparation

In a bowl, mix oatmeal with boiled and mashed potatoes.

Add grated carrot, chopped onion, pressed garlic, cumin, paprika, salt, pepper and tomato paste. Mix well. Add flour to bind the mixture and give it a pliable consistency.

Form small portions of the mixture and press into flat patties.

Heat oil in a pan and fry the vegetable patties on both sides until golden brown.

Drain on paper towels to remove excess oil.

Serve the vegetable patties with your choice of side dishes or in a burger.

Tomato and Pepper Rice dish (Portugal)

Ingredients

1 cup (200 g) long grain rice

2 tbsp olive oil

of garlic, chopped 2 red peppers, diced

4 ripe tomatoes, diced

1 teaspoon paprika powder

Fresh parsley for garnish

2 cups water

1 onion, finely chopped 2 cloves

1 teaspoon tomato paste

Salt and pepper

Preparation

Rinse the rice thoroughly and cook in a pot with 2 cups of water until cooked. Put aside.

Heat the olive oil in a pan and fry the chopped onion until golden brown.

Add the minced garlic and sauté briefly until fragrant.

Add the diced peppers to the pan and sauté over medium heat until softened, about 5 minutes.

Add the diced tomatoes, tomato paste and paprika powder. Salt and pepper to taste. Simmer until the tomatoes break down and the mixture reaches a thick consistency, about 10 minutes.

Mix the cooked rice into the vegetable mixture and mix well. Garnish the dish with fresh parsley and serve.

Kaiserschmarrn (Austria)

Ingredients

180 g flour
1 packet of baking powder
2 tbsp agave syrup
3 tbsp (rapeseed) oil for the dough

350 ml soy milk
1 packet of vanilla sugar
1 pinch of salt
3 tbsp (rapeseed) oil for frying

Preparation

Mix all ingredients in a bowl until a smooth dough forms
Heat oil in a pan.
Pour the dough into the pan and fry on medium heat.
Remove from the edge every now and then and turn the entire dough when the underside is fried and the dough is no longer liquid on top.
Continue frying briefly and then divide the dough into small pieces.
If necessary, add a little more oil and fry the pieces until crispy.
Dust with powdered sugar and serve.

White Bean Stew (Bulgaria)

Ingredients
250 g white beans (canned, drained and washed)

500 ml water	1 tomato, chopped small
1 pepper, diced	1 carrot, diced
1 onion, chopped	1 clove of garlic, pressed
2 tsp mint	1 tsp savory
1 teaspoon salt	1 teaspoon pepper
1 pinch of baking soda	2 tbsp flour
1 tbsp paprika powder	4 tbsp (rapeseed) oil for frying

Side dish: white bread

Preparation
Boil the beans with water in the pot and add baking soda. Simmer the beans until soft for an hour. Once the beans are tender but still slightly al dente, add the chopped onions, garlic, carrots and peppers and cook for another 10 minutes. Stir in the tomatoes and salt and simmer for another 5 minutes. Add the spices, except the paprika powder, and let the soup steep. Heat the oil and flour in a second pot, stirring constantly with a whisk. Add paprika powder and stir until there are no lumps left. Deglaze the soup with a ladle, stir well and add the contents of the second pot to the first. Bring the soup pot to the boil again and serve with white bread

South Tyrolean Spinach Dumplings (Italy)

Ingredients (6 dumplings)

250 g – 300 g dumpling bread (or rolls from the day before)
300 g frozen spinach, drained   250 ml soy milk
3 tbsp soy flour, mixed in 100 ml water
80 g onions   1 clove of garlic
1 teaspoon salt   2 pinches pepper
20 ml (rapeseed) oil for frying   3 tbsp yeast flakes
Sauce:
200 g vegan butter   3 tbsp yeast flakes

Preparation

Place the dumpling bread in a large bowl (cut the old rolls into small pieces).

Dice the onions and press the garlic finely and fry them in a pan with oil until translucent. Add spinach and bring to the boil.

Add soy milk and simmer over medium heat for 2 minutes.

Fold in soy flour, salt, pepper and yeast flakes and stir well.

Add everything to the bowl with the dumpling bread and let cool slightly. Mix and form dumplings. Let the dumplings sit in a pot of gently simmering salted water for 20 minutes. Slowly heat the butter in a saucepan. When the butter is liquid, add the yeast flakes.

Place the dumplings on a plate and serve with the sauce poured over them.

Potato Gratin (France)

Ingredients

1 kg potatoes (preferably waxy)
250 g plant cream
3 pinches of nutmeg
Salt and pepper to taste

150 g plant milk
50 g vegan butter

Preparation

Preheat oven to 180 degrees C fan oven.
Grease the baking dish with a little vegan butter.
Cut the peeled and washed potato into thin slices.
Arrange the potato slices in the baking dish and season each layer with salt, pepper and a little nutmeg.
Mix the cream with the plant milk and pour over the potatoes.
Dice the remaining butter into small cubes and spread over the gratin.
Bake in the oven for 45 minutes until the potatoes are golden brown and the liquid has absorbed.

Couscous with Chickpeas (Morocco)

Ingredients

250 g couscous	2 carrots, diced
1 can of chickpeas (approx. 400 g), rinsed and drained	
2 zucchini, diced	1 red pepper, diced
1 onion, finely chopped	2 cloves of garlic, minced
3 tbsp olive oil	1 tsp cumin
1 teaspoon cinnamon (optional)	1 teaspoon saffron threads
Salt and pepper to taste	500 ml vegetable stock

Preparation

Heat the olive oil in a large pot. Saute onion and garlic until soft. Add the diced vegetables and sauté until lightly browned, about 5 minutes.

Add chickpeas, cumin, cinnamon and optional saffron. Mix well.

Add the couscous and pour over the vegetable broth. Cover the pot and remove from the heat. Let it sit for about 10 minutes until the couscous has absorbed the liquid.

Fluff the couscous with a fork and season with salt and pepper.

Garnish with fresh herbs such as parsley or coriander if desired.

Grilled Green Asparagus (Spain)

Ingredients

500 g green asparagus
2 tbsp olive oil
Sea salt to taste

Preparation

Wash the green asparagus and cut off the woody ends.

Preheat a grill pan or grill.

Drizzle the asparagus with olive oil, making sure it is evenly coated.

Place the asparagus on the hot grill and grill until tender and lightly browned, about 5-7 minutes. Turn occasionally.

Sprinkle with sea salt and serve immediately.

Fried Rice (Vietnam)

Ingredients

250 g cooked long grain rice (preferably from the day before)
200 g firm tofu, diced   2 spring onions, chopped
1 cup mixed vegetables (carrots, peas, corn, peppers), finely diced
3 cloves of garlic, minced   2 tbsp soy sauce
1 tbsp sesame oil   1 tsp ginger, grated
1 teaspoon paprika powder   salt and pepper
2 tablespoons rapeseed oil for frying

Preparation

Loosen the cooked rice so that there are no lumps. Rice from the day before is ideal as it is a little drier.

Heat the vegetable oil in a large pan. Briefly fry the garlic and ginger until fragrant. Add tofu and fry until golden brown. Add the vegetables and fry for 3-5 minutes until soft. Add the rice to the pan and mix well.

Add soy sauce, sesame oil and paprika powder. Mix everything thoroughly and continue frying until the rice is slightly crispy.

Season with salt and pepper.

Garnish with chopped spring onions and serve immediately.

Vegetable Stew "Chakalaka" (South Africa)

Ingredients

1 can of beans baked in tomato sauce

2 carrots

2 onions

3 teaspoons curry

1 teaspoon pepper

Side dish: rice

3 peppers

1 teaspoon vegetable broth

1 teaspoon salt

4 tablespoons rapeseed oil for frying

Preparation

Cut the peppers and carrots into 1 cm cubes. Chop the onion finely.

Heat the oil in a pan and simmer the vegetables for 15 minutes on a low heat, stirring frequently.

Add the beans and remaining ingredients and simmer on a low level for another 15 minutes. Stir again and again.

Serve vegetables with rice.

Tempeh Pan (Indonesia)

Ingredients

400 g tempeh, diced
200 g sprouts
10 spring onions, sliced
1 pepper, diced
2 teaspoons pepper
5 tbsp rapeseed oil
5 tbsp soy sauce and as desired to taste
Side dish: rice

200 g mushrooms, sliced
2 carrots, sliced

4 cloves of garlic, finely chopped
2 teaspoons chili powder

Preparation

Heat oil in a large pan or wok and fry tempeh over medium heat for 5 minutes.
Add mushrooms, peppers and spring onions.
Stir frequently over medium heat for 5 minutes.
Add the paprika, garlic cloves, pepper, chili powder and 5 tablespoons of soy sauce and continue to simmer for 3 minutes, stirring constantly.
Fold in the sprouts and remove the pan from the heat.
Stir in a little more soy sauce if desired and serve with rice.

Rösti with Vegetables (Switzerland)

Ingredients

500 g waxy potatoes
1 carrot, grated
2 tablespoons vegetable oil

1 onion, finely chopped
1 zucchini, grated
Salt and pepper

Preparation

Peel the potatoes and grate them coarsely.

Place the grated potatoes in a clean kitchen towel and squeeze out excess liquid.

Add the chopped onion, grated carrot and zucchini to the potatoes. Mix well.

Heat the vegetable oil in a large pan.

Pour the vegetable and potato mixture into the pan and spread it evenly, pressing lightly.

Fry over medium heat until golden brown. After about 8-10 minutes, turn and fry the other side until crispy.

Season with salt and pepper.

Cut the rosti into pieces and serve immediately.

Glass Noodles "Japchae" (Korea)

Ingredients

200 g glass noodles
1 carrot, cut into strips
2 cloves garlic, minced
1 tbsp sesame oil
2 tbsp rapeseed oil

1 handful of spinach, washed
1 onion, chopped
2 tbsp soy sauce
1 tbsp sugar
Sesame seeds for garnish

Preparation

Cook the glass noodles according to the package instructions, drain and rinse. Put aside.

Heat the vegetable oil in a pan. Fry onions and garlic until soft.

Add carrot strips and continue frying until soft.

Add spinach and stir until wilted.

Add the cooked glass noodles to the pan.

Add soy sauce, sesame oil and sugar. Mix everything well and continue frying until the noodles are warmed through.

Garnish with sesame seeds and serve.

Braised White Cabbage (Ukraine)

Ingredients

1 medium white cabbage, chopped
3 tomatoes, diced
Salt and pepper to taste.
Side dish: rice

2 onions, chopped
3 tablespoons rapeseed oil
Fresh herbs to garnish

Preparation

Heat oil in a large pot. Sauté onions until soft.

Add the chopped white cabbage and stir-fry until softened, about 10 minutes.

Stir in the diced tomatoes and simmer for another 5 minutes.

Season with salt and pepper. Cover the pot and simmer the dish over low heat until all the flavors have melded together, about 15-20 minutes.

Serve with rice as a side dish and garnished with fresh herbs.

Massaman Curry (Thailand)

Ingredients

200 g firm tofu, cut into cubes
2 potatoes, peeled and cut into cubes
1 can (400 ml) coconut milk
1 cinnamon stick
2 tbsp peanut butter
1 tbsp brown sugar
Fresh coriander for garnish
Side dish: rice

80 g peanuts
1 onion, chopped
2 tbsp massaman curry paste
½ tsp cardamom
1 tbsp soy sauce
1 tbsp rapeseed oil

Preparation

Heat oil in a large pot and fry onion until soft.
Add the Massaman curry paste and fry briefly.
Add coconut milk, cinnamon stick and cardamom. Mix well.
Add the potatoes, peanuts and tofu cubes to the pot. Bring everything to a boil and then reduce the heat.
Add peanut butter, soy sauce and brown sugar. Stir well and simmer the curry for about 20-25 minutes until the potatoes are tender.
Garnish with fresh coriander and serve with rice.

Tofu Noodles with Teriyaki Sauce (Japan)

Ingredients

200 g tofu, diced

1 carrot, cut into strips

2 spring onions, cut into rings

3 tbsp teriyaki sauce

1 tbsp sesame oil

200 g Asian noodles

2 cloves of garlic, minced

2 tbsp soy sauce

1 tbsp rapeseed oil

Sesame seeds and spring onions for garnish

Preparation

Cook the pasta according to the instructions on the package. Drain and set aside.

Heat oil in a pan. Fry the diced tofu until golden brown. Remove and set aside.

In the same oil, fry the chopped garlic until fragrant. Add the carrot and fry briefly.

Add the cooked noodles and tofu cubes to the pan. Add teriyaki sauce, soy sauce and sesame oil. Mix everything well and heat.

Stir in the spring onions and continue to fry until the vegetables and tofu are well coated.

Garnish with sesame seeds and additional green onions.

Mac 'n' Cheese (USA)

Ingredients

300 g macaroni
100 g carrots, diced
30 g yeast flakes (for a cheesy taste)
60 g vegetable margarine
½ teaspoon mustard

200 g potatoes, diced
75 g cashews
juice of half a lemon
1 garlic clove, chopped
Salt and pepper to taste

Preparation

Cook the pasta according to the instructions on the package. Drain and set aside.

Cook the diced potatoes, carrots and cashews in a pot of water until soft.

Drain the cooked vegetables and cashews, reserving about 1 cup of the cooking water.

In a blender or food processor, puree the cooked vegetables, cashews, nutritional yeast, vegetable margarine, garlic, mustard, lemon juice, salt and pepper. Add reserved cooking water as needed to reach desired consistency.

Pour the sauce over the cooked pasta and mix well.

Season with additional spices if desired and serve.

Sauces, Dips, Dressings and Spreads

Tempting aromas and savory delicacies to pamper your taste buds: Start your day with delicious sauces, dips and spreads that offer a wealth of purely plant-based delights!

Hummus (Syria)

Ingredients

300 g dry chickpeas
300 g sesame paste (tahini)
4 cloves of garlic
2 pinches of salt
1 teaspoon paprika powder

100 ml rapeseed oil
Juice of 4 lemons
1 teaspoon of pepper
1 teaspoon cumin

Preparation

Soak chickpeas overnight.
The next day, drain and cook until soft.
Do not drain the water.
Puree the chickpeas with a hand blender.
Add sesame paste and puree together again.
Add the garlic, spices and lemon juice.
Place hummus on a deeper plate.
Heat the oil and spread over the hummus.

Peanut Butter (USA)

Ingredients

400 g roasted peanuts (unsalted)
30 ml almond milk
½ tsp salt

Preparation

Puree all ingredients in the blender to a creamy mass.
The peanut butter will last up to 14 days in the refrigerator

Alioli (Spain)

Ingredients

6 cloves of garlic
50 ml sunflower oil
1 tsp lemon juice

50 ml olive oil
1 teaspoon salt

Preparation

Puree the garlic cloves with salt.
Slowly add olive oil and sunflower oil, stirring constantly.
Stir in lemon juice and chill until ready to use.

Guacamole (Mexico)

Ingredients

3 ripe avocados
2 tomatoes, diced
A handful of fresh coriander, chopped
Salt and pepper to taste

1 small onion, finely chopped
1 garlic clove, finely chopped
Juice of one lime

Preparation

Halve the avocados, remove the stone and scoop the flesh into a bowl with a spoon.
Mash the avocados with a fork until a creamy consistency is achieved.
Add onion, tomatoes, coriander and garlic and mix well.
Squeeze the lime juice over it and season with salt and pepper.
Allow the guacamole to steep briefly in the refrigerator before serving.

Muhammara (Syrian)

Ingredients

200 g walnuts
3 red peppers
6 tbsp olive oil
1 pinch of salt

5 slices of rusks
2 cloves of garlic
2 tbsp harissa (opt. sambal olek)

Preparation

Quarter the peppers and put them in a bowl with all the ingredients.
Puree with a hand blender or in a blender to a creamy paste.
Place in a small bowl.
The pepper paste lasts at least 2 days in the refrigerator, or you can also freeze it.

Macadamia Mint Pesto (Australia)

Ingredients

150 g macadamia nuts
A handful of fresh mint leaves
Salt to taste

2 cloves of garlic
120 ml olive oil

Preparation

Lightly toast the macadamia nuts in a pan until golden brown.
Place mint leaves, toasted macadamia nuts, garlic and salt in a blender.
Add olive oil and puree everything to a creamy consistency.
Season to taste and pour into a glass.

Vegan Liver Sausage (Germany)

Ingredients

200 g brown lentils, cooked
1 onion, chopped
60 ml rapeseed oil
1 teaspoon caraway
1 teaspoon paprika powder (sweet)
Salt and pepper to taste

100 g smoked tofu, diced
2 cloves of garlic, chopped
1 tsp marjoram

Preparation

Roughly mash the cooked lentils in a large bowl.

In a pan, fry the onion and garlic in rapeseed oil until translucent.

Add the steamed onions and garlic to the lentils and mix well.

Add marjoram, caraway, paprika powder, salt and pepper. Season well and mix.

Fold in the diced smoked tofu and mix again.

Pour the mixture into a preserving jar and let it steep in the refrigerator for at least 2 hours so that the flavors develop well.

Greek Feta

Ingredients

400 g natural tofu
1 teaspoon thyme
3 teaspoons salt
2 pinches of pepper
Water

100 ml olive oil
1 teaspoon basil
1 teaspoon lemon juice
2 pinches of salt

Preparation

Dry the tofu and cut it into small cubes.
Boil water in a pot.
Add tofu cubes and simmer on medium heat for 10 minutes.
Drain the tofu in a sieve and place in a sealable jar.
Sprinkle tofu with herbs and spices and pour lemon juice over it.
Fill the glass with olive oil.
Leave closed in the fridge for 3 days.
The vegan feta will then last for 5 days.

Greek Tzatziki

Ingredients

500 g natural soy yogurt
2 cloves of garlic
1 tbsp (olive) oil
1 teaspoon salt
Optional 2 tsp ground psyllium husks

1 cucumber
2 tbsp dill
1 tsp lemon juice
1 teaspoon pepper

Preparation

Press garlic cloves.

Halve the cucumber, remove the seeds and grate coarsely.

Mix all ingredients in a bowl and let sit for 3 hours.

If you like the tzatziki firmer, you can also add 2 teaspoons of ground psyllium husk while stirring.

Italian Pesto

Ingredients

50 g pine nuts
40 g basil
4 tbsp olive oil.
¼ tsp pepper

50 g walnut kernels
½ tsp salt
2 tbsp yeast flakes
Optional: 1 clove of garlic

Preparation

Place the pine nuts and walnuts in a heated pan and sauté for 2 minutes, turning frequently.

Put the kernels with all the ingredients in a bowl and process them into a fine mass using a hand blender.

Store the pesto in an airtight container in the refrigerator. Stir well before serving with pasta, on bread or as a dip.

Gochujang Sauce (Korea)

Ingredients

3 tbsp gochujang (Korean fermented chili paste)
2 tbsp rice vinegar
1 garlic clove, minced
1 tbsp maple syrup or agave syrup
2 tbsp soy sauce (or tamari for gluten-free)
1 tsp grated fresh ginger
Optional: spring onions, finely chopped, as a garnish

Preparation

In a bowl, combine gochujang, rice vinegar, minced garlic, maple syrup, soy sauce and freshly grated ginger.
Mix all ingredients well until a uniform mixture is formed.
Taste the sauce and adjust the sweetness or spiciness if necessary.
Optionally garnish with finely chopped spring onions.
Let the gochujang sauce steep for at least 15-20 minutes before serving so that the flavors develop well.

Arrabbiata Sauce (Italy)

Ingredients

800 g tomatoes, diced (canned or fresh)
3 garlic cloves, minced
2 tablespoons olive oil
1 tsp dried chili flakes
Salt and pepper
A handful of fresh parsley, chopped

Preparation

Heat the olive oil in a saucepan over medium heat. Add the minced garlic and chili flakes. Sauté gently until the garlic is fragrant but not brown.

Add the diced tomatoes to the pot. Season with salt and pepper.

Bring the sauce to a boil, then reduce the heat and simmer for about 15-20 minutes. Stir occasionally.

Mix the chopped parsley into the sauce and simmer for a few more minutes.

Season with additional salt and pepper.

Sate Sauce (Indonesia)

Ingredients

150 g peanut butter
2 tbsp soy sauce
2 tbsp brown sugar
1 garlic clove, minced

200 ml coconut milk
juice of one lime
1 tsp ginger, grated
1 teaspoon sesame oil (optional)

Preparation

In a small saucepan, combine peanut butter, coconut milk, soy sauce, lime juice, brown sugar, ginger and garlic.

Cook over medium heat, stirring constantly, until peanut butter is melted and ingredients are well combined.

Add sesame oil if desired and continue stirring.

Simmer the sauce over low heat until slightly thickened.

Taste and add additional soy sauce, sugar or lime juice as needed.

Allow the satay sauce to cool and serve with satay skewers, vegetables, pasta or rice.

Curry Coconut Sauce (India)

Ingredients

400 ml coconut milk
2-3 tbsp curry paste
2 tbsp soy sauce

2 cloves of garlic, chopped
1 tbsp ginger, grated

Preparation

In a pan or pot, mix the curry paste with a little coconut milk and heat over medium heat until the flavors develop.
Add garlic and ginger and sauté briefly until fragrant.
Stir in the remaining coconut milk and add the soy sauce. Mix well.
Simmer the sauce over low heat until it thickens slightly.
Taste and adjust as needed.

Bread and Buns

Delicious aromas and filling pleasures that will enchant your taste buds: Start your day with delicious bread and roll creations made from purely plant-based ingredients!

Baguette (France)

Ingredients (2 baguettes)

200 g flour, type 405
300 ml water, cold
3 pinches of salt
1 tsp vegetable oil

200 g spelled flour, type 630
¼ tsp dry yeast
1 pinch of sugar

Preparation

Mix flour, dry yeast, salt, sugar and oil.

Mix in cold water and knead a dough.

Let the dough stand covered for at least 12 hours.

Preheat oven to 180 degrees C fan oven.

Form the dough into two baguettes and place them on a baking tray lined with baking paper.

Place an oven-safe bowl of water under the baking tray.

Bake for 20 minutes. When the baguettes are nice and brown, remove them from the oven.

Ciabatta (Italy)

Ingredients (2 ciabatta)

500 g flour, type 405
½ tsp dry yeast
1 teaspoon sugar

350 ml water, lukewarm
2 tsp salt
2 tablespoons olive oil

Preparation

Mix all ingredients into a smooth dough.

Cover the dough and let it rise overnight.

Form 2 ciabatta loaves on a baking tray lined with baking paper. Dust lightly with flour and let rise for 30 minutes.

Preheat oven to 180 degrees C fan oven.

Bake in the oven for 30 minutes.

The ciabatta should be eaten within 2 days.

Of course, you can also freeze it.

Swiss Bürli

Ingredients

400 g wheat flour
340 ml lukewarm water
2 tsp salt

100 g rye flour
½ cube yeast

Preparation

Dissolve yeast in the water and mix with the remaining ingredients.
Cover the dough and let it rise overnight for at least 12 hours.
Preheat oven to 180 degrees C fan oven.
Take the dough out of the fridge, lightly flour it and scoop out 12 bulbs with a tablespoon.
Place the Bürlis on a baking tray lined with baking paper and let them bake for 25 minutes.
Do a stick test. If the dough still sticks, add some time.
Let the rolls cool on a wire rack.

Indian Naan Rolls

Ingredients

450 g flour
3 tbsp plant milk
2 teaspoons garlic powder
1 tbsp sugar
1 tbsp (rapeseed) oil

250 ml lukewarm water
1/2 packet dry yeast
1 teaspoon curry powder
1 tsp salt

Preparation

Dissolve yeast in warm water and let stand for 10 minutes.

Add remaining ingredients and knead into a soft dough.

Let the dough rise covered for 1 hour.

Then divide the dough into golf ball-sized pieces and let it rest, covered, for another 30 minutes.

Roll out the dough balls thinly and fry in a pan on the highest level for 2 minutes until bubbles form and the naan bread turns slightly brown.

Mexican Tortillas

Ingredients (6 tortillas)

250 g wheat flour (type 405)　　250 ml boiling water
½ tsp salt　　50 g flour for rolling

Preparation

Put the flour and salt in a bowl and make a well in the middle.

Pour in the boiling water, stirring constantly.

Knead the hot dough.

Lightly flour the work surface and divide the dough into six portions and roll out into tortillas.

Fry in a coated pan without oil for a minute on each side.

Rolls (Germany)

Ingredients

500 g wheat flour (Type 550)   300 ml lukewarm water
1 packet of dry yeast or 42 g of fresh yeast
1 teaspoon sugar   1 teaspoon salt
2 tbsp vegetable oil

Preparation

Sift the flour into a large bowl and form a well in the center. Pour yeast into the well, sprinkle sugar over it and mix with lukewarm water.

Allow the yeast to activate for 5-10 minutes (this step can be omitted with dry yeast).

Add salt, remaining water and vegetable oil and knead everything into a smooth dough.

Knead the dough on a floured surface for another 10 minutes until it is elastic and no longer sticky. Form into a ball, place in a lightly oiled bowl, cover and let rise for 1 hour or until doubled in size. Degas the dough on a floured surface and divide into 8-10 pieces. Form each into a ball, place on a baking tray lined with baking paper, cover and let rest for another 15-20 minutes. Preheat oven to 220 degrees Celsius. Cut rolls as needed and bake for 15-20 minutes, until golden brown.

Remove from the oven and let cool on a wire rack.

Chinese Mantou

Ingredients

500 g wheat flour
50 g sugar
1 teaspoon Baking powder

10 g dry yeast
250 ml warm water

Preparation

In a bowl, dissolve dry yeast in warm water, add sugar and stir well until sugar is completely dissolved. Let the mixture sit for 5-10 minutes until it becomes foamy.

In a large bowl, sift the flour. Make a well in the center and pour the yeast mixture into it. Carefully push the flour from the edge to the center, gradually incorporating the yeast mixture until a dough forms. Knead the dough on a floured surface until smooth. Place back in the bowl, cover with a clean tea towel and let rise in a warm place until doubled in size, about 1-2 hours. Knead the dough again to remove air bubbles and cut in half. Shape each half of the dough into a cylinder and cut into slices about 2 cm thick. Place each slice on a square piece of parchment paper and steam using a steamer or in a steamer basket for 15-20 minutes until the mantou are puffy and firm.

Serve warm and enjoy with soy sauce or other dips if desired.

English Scones

Ingredients

250 g wheat flour   50 g sugar
1 tbsp baking powder   ½ tsp salt
115g unsalted vegan butter, cold and diced
160 ml plant milk   1 teaspoon vanilla extract
60 g raisins (optional)

Preparation

Preheat the oven to 220 °C top/bottom heat and line a baking tray with baking paper.
Mix flour, sugar, baking powder and salt in a bowl.
Add cold butter to dry mixture until coarse crumbs form.
plant milk and vanilla extract in a separate bowl.
Pour milk mixture into well of dry ingredients and stir gently until combined. Optional: incorporate raisins/currants.
Knead the dough briefly on a floured surface and shape it into a 2.5 cm thick circle.
Cut out the scones and place them on the baking tray.
Bake for 12-15 minutes until golden brown. Let cool on a rack.

Turkish Flatbread

Ingredients

500 g wheat flour
1 cube yeast
1 teaspoon black cumin (or sesame)
1 pinch of sugar

200 ml lukewarm water
5 tsp olive oil
1 teaspoon salt

Preparation

Place the flour in a bowl and make a well in it.

Crumble in the yeast, add sugar and mix with 150 ml lukewarm water. Dust the pre-dough with a little flour, cover it with a cloth and let it rise in a warm place for 30 minutes.

Then add the remaining water, salt and 3 tablespoons of oil and knead a smooth dough. Dust with flour and let the dough rest again, covered, in a warm place for 30 minutes.

Preheat oven to 180 degrees C fan oven.

Knead the dough well again, divide into 2 portions and form elongated flat cakes.

Use your fingers to make longitudinal and transverse grooves in the dough and pull up the edges of the dough slightly.

Brush the flatbreads with the remaining oil and sprinkle with black cumin. Let rest for 15 minutes. Place the flatbreads on a baking tray lined with baking paper and let them bake for 25 minutes.

Greek Pita

Ingredients

350 g wheat flour
1 teaspoon sugar
1 packet of dry yeast

1 teaspoon salt
1 tablespoon olive oil
225 ml lukewarm water

Preparation

In a large bowl, mix the wheat flour with salt.

In a small bowl, dissolve dry yeast and sugar in lukewarm water. Let sit until bubbles form, about 5 minutes.

Add the yeast mixture to the flour and add olive oil. Mix well and knead into a smooth dough. Knead the dough on a lightly floured surface until elastic, about 8-10 minutes.

Place the dough ball back in the bowl, cover with a clean towel and let rise in a warm place until doubled in size, about 1 hour. Knead the dough again on a floured surface and divide into 6 equal pieces of dough.

Shape each piece of dough into a ball and roll it out on a floured surface into thin flat cakes (approx. 20 cm in diameter).

Preheat a skillet over medium heat. Bake the pita flatbreads individually in the pan for about 1-2 minutes per side until they are bubbling and lightly browned.

Keep the finished pita breads warm until they are all baked.

Desserts and Sweets

Pamper your taste buds with heavenly desserts and sweet delicacies made from purely plant-based ingredients that will sweeten your day with delicate flavors and satisfying pleasures!

Oat Cookies (Sweden)

Ingredients (approx. 30 cookies)

120 g crunchy oat flakes
100 g vegan butter
100 g flour
½ teaspoon baking powder

50 g chopped almonds
120 g sugar
1 packet of vanilla sugar

Preparation

Preheat oven to 180 degrees C fan oven.

Melt the vegan butter for the dough.

Stir in the oat flakes and let cool slightly.

Add the remaining ingredients and knead into a soft dough.

Using two teaspoons, place small portions on a baking tray lined with baking paper and flatten them slightly.

Bake in the oven for 15 minutes.

Waffles (Belgium)

Ingredients (8 waffles)

500 ml soy milk

1 packet of vanilla sugar

6 tbsp sugar

1 pinch of salt

500 g flour

1 packet of baking powder

Zest from an organic lemon peel

4 tbsp (rapeseed) oil for baking

Preparation

Mix all the ingredients with a whisk to form a slightly liquid dough.

Preheat the waffle iron.

When ready, brush with oil and place about 1 1/2 ladles into the waffle iron.

Bake for 3 minutes and then open carefully. If you notice that the dough is slightly sticking to the top iron, carefully loosen it with a knife.

Oil the waffle iron again and pour in the next ladle.

Top or sprinkle finished waffles as desired.

Crepes (France)

Ingredients (8 crepes)

250 ml soy milk
1 packet of vanilla sugar
1 tbsp agave syrup
2 tbsp vegetable oil for frying

250 g flour
250 g mineral water
1 pinch of salt

Preparation

Mix all the ingredients with a whisk to form a slightly liquid dough.
Let the dough stand covered for at least an hour.
Brush a pan with oil and heat it up.
Pour half a ladle of batter into the pan.
Swirl the pan and distribute the batter evenly.
Fry the crepes until golden brown.
Fill or top as desired.

American Pancakes

Ingredients

150 g flour
200 g soy yogurt
1 packet of baking powder
1 pinch of salt

50 g soy flour
100 ml soy milk
2 tablespoons of agave syrup
3 tablespoons rapeseed oil for frying

Preparation

Mix all dry ingredients in a bowl.
Add the liquid ingredients and stir in.
Heat oil in a pan and pour in 3 tablespoons of batter.
Fry the pancakes over medium heat until golden brown on both sides.

Almond Tartlets (Spain)

Ingredients (8 pieces)

400 ml almond milk
100 g chopped almond
200 g flour
150 g sugar
3 tbsp flax seeds
2 pinches of cinnamon
Vegan butter for greasing

200 g ground almonds
90 g almond butter
130 g vegan butter
Grated zest of an orange
2 tsp orange juice
1 pinch of salt

Preparation

Preheat oven to 180 degrees C fan oven.
Heat almond milk with lei seeds in a pot and let it swell for 10 minutes.
Add the almond butter, butter and orange peel and heat through.
Gradually stir in remaining ingredients.
Grease tartlet tins with butter and spread the dough into them.
Bake for 25 minutes. Use a chopstick to test whether the tartlets are done.
Allow finished tartlets to cool.

American Lemon Donuts

Ingredients (12 donuts)

200 g flour
150 g apple syrup
80 g powdered sugar
5 tbsp applesauce
1/2 tsp baking powder
2 organic lemons
100 ml rapeseed oil for baking

250 ml almond milk
120 g grated almonds
2 tablespoons vegan butter
1 packet vanilla sugar
1 pinch of baking soda
1 pinch of salt

Preparation

Preheat oven to 180 degrees C fan oven.

Grease 12 – 16 donut molds (number depending on the size of the molds) with butter and place them on a baking tray. Grate the lemon peel and squeeze out the juice. Mix flour, almonds, baking soda, salt and baking powder in a bowl. In a second bowl, stir together the applesauce, apple syrup, vanilla sugar, oil, almond milk, half of the lemon zest and a good half of the lemon juice.

Slowly stir the contents of the second bowl into the first bowl.

Divide the dough into the donut tins and bake for 25 minutes.

Mix the powdered sugar with the remaining lemon juice and lemon zest and brush it over the cooled donuts.

Sweet Couscous (North Africa)

Ingredients

400 g couscous, prepared according to the package instructions

8 dates (pitted) — 1 pomegranate

5 tbsp raisins — Hot water

4 tbsp almond flakes — 3 tbsp vegan butter

3 tbsp orange juice — 4 tsp cinnamon

2 tbsp agave syrup — 1 pinch of salt

4 tablespoons powdered sugar for garnish

Preparation

Put the raisins in a bowl and pour hot water over them and let them soak.

Remove the red fruit seeds from the pomegranate and cut the dates into eighths.

Roast the almond flakes in a pan without fat until light brown.

Stir in the butter into the finished couscous.

Drain the raisins and let them drain.

Mix all ingredients, except powdered sugar, with the couscous.

Portion into small, preheated bowls and serve dusted with powdered sugar.

Berry Crumble (England)

Ingredients

300 g mixed berries (e.g. strawberries, raspberries, blueberries)

60 g almond flour
90 g oat flakes
60 g maple syrup or agave syrup
pinch of salt

60 g coconut oil, melted
1 tbsp lemon juice
¼ teaspoon cinnamon

Preparation

Preheat the oven to 180°C and grease a baking dish.

Put the mixed berries in the mold and mix with lemon juice and maple syrup.

In a separate bowl, stir together the oats, almond flour, melted coconut oil, cinnamon and salt until crumbly.

Sprinkle the crumble mixture evenly over the berries.

Bake the berry crumble for about 30 minutes, until the berries are juicy and the crumbs are golden brown.

Remove from oven and allow to cool slightly.

Serve the berry crumble warm or at room temperature and garnish with vegan yogurt if desired.

Chocolate Chia Pudding (Australia)

Ingredients

250 g plant milk (e.g. almond milk or oat milk)
4 tbsp chia seeds   2 tbsp cocoa powder
2 tsp maple syrup   1 tsp vanilla sugar
Toppings of your choice (e.g. berries, nuts, coconut flakes)

Preparation

In a bowl, combine chia seeds, cocoa powder, maple syrup and vanilla extract.

Add the plant milk and stir thoroughly to avoid lumps.

Place the pudding in the refrigerator for at least 2 hours or overnight to allow the chia seeds to swell and create a pudding-like consistency.

Then pour the chocolate chia pudding into glasses or bowls and garnish with toppings as desired.

Serve the pudding chilled.

Panna Cotta (Italy)

Ingredients

600 ml coconut milk
1 packet of vanilla pudding powder
4 tbsp sugar

4 tbsp desiccated coconut
2 teaspoons of agar - agar

Preparation

Bring all ingredients to the boil in a pot while stirring.
Simmer over medium heat for 2 minutes, stirring.
Divide the panna cotta into glasses and place in the refrigerator for at least 1 hour.

Brownies (USA)

Ingredients

150 g flour
1 teaspoon baking powder
200 g sugar
240 ml almond milk
50 g cocoa powder
½ teaspoon salt
120 ml rapeseed oil
1 teaspoon vanilla sugar
100 g vegan chocolate (chopped or chocolate chips)

Preparation

Preheat the oven to 180°C and line a baking pan with baking paper.

In a bowl, mix the flour, cocoa powder, baking powder and salt.

In another bowl, mix the sugar, vegetable oil, vegetable milk and vanilla extract well.

Add the dry ingredients to the wet ingredients and mix until smooth. Fold the chopped vegan chocolate into the dough. Pour the batter evenly into the prepared baking pan and smooth it out.

Bake the brownies in the preheated oven for about 25-30 minutes, until a toothpick comes out clean (a few moist crumbs are okay).

Remove the brownies from the oven and allow them to cool completely in the tin before cutting into squares.

Mousse au Chocolat (France)

Ingredients

200 g vegan dark chocolate

Drain water "Aquafaba" from 2 cans of chickpeas

1 packet of baking powder	4 teaspoons of powdered sugar

2 pinches of salt

Preparation

Melt the chocolate in a water bath.

In the meantime, collect the liquid from 2 cans of chickpeas and beat with baking powder.

When the cream is almost ready, stir in the powdered sugar and salt.

Let the chocolate cool until it is lukewarm.

Fold in the chocolate with a whisk.

Divide the mousse into bowls and place in the refrigerator for 30 minutes.

By the way: Auqafaba can also be frozen easily

Dulce de Leche (Argentina)

Ingredients

1 can (approx. 400 ml) unsweetened coconut milk
200 g brown sugar
1 teaspoon vanilla sugar

Preparation

Put all ingredients in a pot.
Bring the mixture to a boil over medium heat and then reduce the heat.
Stirring occasionally, simmer the mixture over low heat until thick and caramelized, about 40 minutes.
Be careful not to burn the mixture and stir regularly.
Once the desired consistency is reached, remove the pot from the heat and allow to cool.
Pour the cooled dulce de leche into a jar or airtight container and store in the refrigerator.

Chocolate Ice Cream (Italy)

Ingredients

400 ml coconut milk (from a can)
150 g sugar
1 teaspoon vanilla sugar
Optional: 50 g vegan chocolate (melted)

200 ml plant-based milk
50 g unsweetened cocoa powder
A pinch of salt

Preparation

Mix all the ingredients together well in a bowl until the sugar is completely dissolved.

Pour the mixture into a shallow, freezer-safe bowl or mold.

Cover the bowl and place in the freezer.

Every 30 minutes, fluff the ice cream with a fork and stir to prevent ice crystals from forming. Repeat this process about 3-4 times.

Optional: During the freezing process, gently stir the melted vegan chocolate into the semi-frozen ice cream to add chocolate chips.

Blueberry Cassis – Lassi (India)

Ingredients (6 glasses)

400 g frozen blueberries (blueberries)
400 g silken tofu
60 ml cassis liqueur (optional: blackcurrant syrup)
400 ml cold water
3 tbsp sugar
3 tbsp lemon juice
1 pinch of salt

Preparation

Puree all ingredients in a blender or large bowl with an immersion blender. Serve immediately or chill and puree again before serving.
The lassi can be stored in the refrigerator for up to 2 days.

Popcorn with Caramel Sauce (USA)

Ingredients

50 g popcorn corn
40 g sugar
1 tbsp rapeseed oil

40 g vegan butter
1 tbsp agave syrup
70 g cashews (optional)

Preparation

Heat butter, sugar and agave syrup in a saucepan.

Cook on high for 2 minutes, stirring constantly, then set aside.

(Optional) Roast the cashews in a pan on a medium heat for 4 minutes, stirring until golden brown. Then place it on a plate.

Pop the popcorn corn in a pot with oil according to the instructions. Occasionally shake the pot and hold the lid firmly.

Pour the caramel sauce over the popcorn and cashews and mix well.

Place the popcorn on a baking tray lined with baking paper, spread it out and let it cool.

Only serve when it is thoroughly dry.

Disclaimer

Implementation of all information, instructions and strategies contained in this book is at your own risk. The author cannot accept liability for any damage of any kind for any legal reason. Liability claims against the author are generally excluded for material or immaterial damage caused by the use or non-use of the information or by the use of incorrect and/or incomplete information. Any legal claims and claims for damages are therefore excluded. This work was prepared and written down with the greatest care and to the best of our knowledge and belief. However, the author assumes no liability for the timeliness, completeness and quality of the information. Printing errors and false information cannot be completely ruled out. No legal responsibility or liability in any form can be assumed for incorrect information provided by the author.

Imprint

© Lydia Solotova
2024

1st Edition

All rights reserved

ISBN: 9798876379740

Reprinting, even in excerpts, is not permitted
No part of this work may be reproduced, duplicated or distributed in any form without the written permission of the author.

Contact:
Markus Mägerle, Am Kreisgraben 17, 93104 Riekofen , Germany

Printed in Great Britain
by Amazon